FIRE AND RESCUE SERVICES ACT 2004

EXPLANATORY NOTES

INTRODUCTION

1.   These explanatory notes relate to the Fire and Rescue Services Act 2004, which received Royal Assent on Thursday 22 July 2004. They have been produced by the Office of the Deputy Prime Minister in order to assist the reader in understanding the Act.

2.   The notes need to be read in conjunction with the Act. They are not, and are not meant to be, a comprehensive description of the Act. So where a section or part of a section of the Act does not seem to require any explanation or comment, none is given.

3.   The Act applies to England and Wales only, with the exception of the provisions relating to pensions in Part 4 and consequential provisions and repeals in Schedules 1 and 2 which also apply to Scotland.

BACKGROUND

4.   The main purpose of this Act is to deliver a modernised Fire and Rescue Service that responds to the particular demands of the 21st Century.

5.   The Act repeals the Fire Services Act 1947.

6.   It gives effect to the majority of proposals that require primary legislation in the White Paper *Our Fire and Rescue Service*, published on 30th June 2003.

7.   The White Paper was a Government response to *The Independent Review of the Fire Service* carried out by Sir George Bain and his team, whose report was published on 16th December 2002.

OVERVIEW

8.   The Act covers various aspects of the Fire and Rescue Service and is in seven Parts:

   ˜   Part 1 - Fire and rescue authorities (sections 1 to 5): determines which body is the fire and rescue authority for an area, and provides for the combination of two or more fire and rescue authorities by order.

   ˜   Part 2 - Functions of fire and rescue authorities (sections 6 to 20): sets out the duties and powers of fire and rescue authorities.

   ˜   Part 3 – Administration (sections 21 to 31): provides for the preparation of a Fire and Rescue National Framework setting out the strategic priorities of the Fire and Rescue Service, and for the supervision of fire and rescue authorities. It makes supplementary provision for the Secretary of State to provide equipment and training centres for fire and rescue authorities.

   ˜   Part 4 – Employment (sections 32 to 37): deals with employment by fire and rescue authorities, in particular the creation of negotiating bodies to determine the terms and conditions of employees, and pension schemes.

~ Part 5 – Water supply (sections 38 to 43): imposes duties on fire and rescue authorities and water undertakers to ensure an adequate supply of water for fire-fighting activities.

~ Part 6 – Supplementary (sections 44 to 54 and Schedules 1 and 2): concerns the powers of fire and rescue authority employees to undertake rescue work and investigations, as well as a number of consequential provisions and repeals, including the abolition of the Central Fire Brigades Advisory Council.

~ Part 7 – General (sections 55 to 64): makes general provision in relation to pre-commencement consultation, interpretation, statutory instruments, territorial extent etc.

9.   The term 'brigade' does not appear in the Act   - this reflects a community service structured on the roles of individuals rather than adherence to a rank structure.

TERRITORIAL APPLICATION

10.   The Act devolves the remaining responsibilities for fire and rescue authorities in Wales to the National Assembly for Wales, taking forward the commitment to do so set out in the *Our Fire and Rescue Service* White Paper. The Act has therefore been drafted in liaison and agreement with officials from the Assembly and the Wales Office. As set out in section 62 (Wales), any reference to the "Secretary of State" in Parts 1 to 6 and sections 60 and 61 of the Act should be treated as a   reference to the "National Assembly for Wales", in the Act's application to Wales.

11.   The Act does not repeal the provisions of the Fire Services Act 1947 as they apply in Scotland, which remain in force. The only exceptions to this are the pension provisions in Part 4 of the Act and consequential provisions, which do extend to Scotland as pension policy is a reserved matter and not a devolved issue under the Scotland Act 1998. The Act, therefore, repeals the existing pension provisions in the 1947 Act, and in turn extends the replacement provisions to England, Wales and Scotland.

12.   The Act does not extend to Northern Ireland.

COMMENTARY ON SECTIONS

PART 1: FIRE AND RESCUE AUTHORITIES

Section 1: Fire and rescue authorities

13.   This section defines what is meant in the Act by "fire and rescue authority" which can differ in constitution from area to area. The establishment and membership of metropolitan county fire and civil defence authorities is dealt with in section 26 of, and Schedule 11(2) to, the Local Government Act 1985 (c. 51). The London Fire and Civil Defence Authority became the London Fire and Emergency Planning Authority under the Greater London Authority Act 1999 (c. 29) - see section 328.

Sections 2, 3 and 4: Creation of combined fire and rescue authorities; supplementary; and combined authorities under the Fire Services Act 1947

14.   The existing power in the Fire Services Act 1947 to create combined fire authorities is re-enacted in a modified form to facilitate the establishment of combined fire and rescue authorities either for reasons of economy, efficiency and effectiveness or in the interests of public safety.

EXPLANATORY NOTES

Fire and Rescue Services Act 2004

Chapter 21

£3.00

15. Combination could also occur where fire and rescue authorities themselves submit a proposal to that effect. Combination schemes that have already been made under the Fire Services Act 1947 will continue in force. Such schemes will be subject to the Secretary of State's power to vary or revoke them by order.

16. The Secretary of State will be able to appoint a minority (up to one half minus one) of the members of the combined fire and rescue authorities created under this legislation.

17. In all cases the Secretary of State will be required to consult the fire and rescue authorities affected, the local authorities in the combined area proposed and other persons considered appropriate beforehand. The term "local authority", for the purposes of this Act , is defined in section 57. The Secretary of State will also be required to hold an inquiry before making a combination order, unless the combination is uncontentious or is urgently required in the interests of public safety.

Section 5: Powers of combined fire and rescue authorities

18. Section 5 gives combined fire and rescue authorities the powers which are already available to county fire authorities, the London Fire and Emergency Planning Authority and metropolitan county fire and civil defence authorities under section 111 of the Local Government Act 1972.

PART 2: FUNCTIONS OF FIRE AND RESCUE AUTHORITIES

Core functions

19. Sections 6, 7, 8 and 9 establish the core duties of fire and rescue authorities.

Section 6: Fire safety

20. The Fire and Rescue Service already carries out a wide range of activities to promote community fire safety, with the aim of preventing deaths and injuries in the home and reducing the impact of fire on the community as a whole. This includes fire safety education (especially for vulnerable groups), smoke alarm installation, chip pan safety demonstrations and fire safety checks for householders and others. Many fire and rescue authorities also provide training programmes for young people and work with local businesses, agencies and partnerships (such as crime and disorder partnerships and local strategic partnerships). This work is currently carried out on a discretionary basis and the effect of section 6 is to impose a statutory duty.

Sections 7 and 8: Fires and road traffic accidents

21. Section 7 re-enacts the existing statutory duty for a fire and rescue authority to plan and provide arrangements for fighting fires and protecting life and property from fires within its area. A fire and rescue authority is required to secure the provision of sufficient personnel, services and equipment to deal with all normal circumstances, as well as adequate training. A fire and rescue authority must also put in place effective arrangements for receiving and responding to calls for help and for obtaining information which it needs to carry out its functions; the latter might include, for example, information about the nature and characteristics of buildings within the authority's area or availability of and access to water supplies.

22. Section 8 places a duty on fire and rescue authorities to make provision for rescuing persons from road traffic accidents and for dealing with the aftermath of such accidents. Historically, the risk of fire was the trigger for attendance at such an incident. While advances in vehicle design have seen the incidence of fire following an accident decrease, calls to assist with the rescue of people from wreckage and protect them from harm from spillage of hazardous substances have increased dramatically. A fire and rescue authority is required, therefore, to secure sufficient resources and training to deal with all normal circumstances. A fire and rescue authority must also put in place effective arrangements for receiving and responding to calls for help and for obtaining information to exercise its functions (for example, knowledge of local road and trunk road network).

23. Under sections 7 and 8 fire and rescue authorities must seek to mitigate the damage, or potential damage, to property in exercising their statutory functions. As a consequence, the actions a fire and rescue authority must take in responding to an incident which could damage property should be proportionate to the incident and the risk to life.

Section 9: Emergencies

24. This section empowers the Secretary of State, by order following consultation, to place a duty on fire and rescue authorities to respond to particular types of emergency, as defined by order, such as flooding and terrorist incidents.

25. The Secretary of State can also, by order following consultation, direct fire and rescue authorities as to how they should plan, equip for and respond to such emergencies. This may include, for example, directions as to the deployments of mass decontamination equipment for civil resilience purposes. The intention is to ensure consistency of approach towards emergencies, particularly in response to terrorist incidents.

26. Section 9 also allows the order to require an authority to respond to an emergency that has arisen outside its own area if, for example, it has more appropriate equipment and training than the authority in whose area the emergency has occurred.

27. The term "emergency" is defined in section 58.

Other functions

Section 10: Directions relating to particular fires and emergencies

28. This section enables the Secretary of State to direct a fire and rescue authority to respond to a particular fire or emergency incident in the event of an extreme or unusual event such as a terrorist attack or natural disaster, where there is no time to revise or make an order under section 9, or where a level of central co-ordination is required. Such a direction can require a fire and rescue authority to act outside as well as inside its own area . The Secretary of State can also direct an authority not to take any action in the event of such an emergency if, for example, another fire and rescue authority is better equipped to do so.

Sections 11 and 12: Power to respond to other eventualities; and other services

29. Section 11 replaces section 3(1)(e) of the Fire Services Act 1947, and provides fire and rescue authorities with discretion to equip and respond to events beyond its core functions provided for elsewhere in the Act. A fire and rescue authority will be free to act where it believes there is a risk to life or the environment. This would allow, for example, a fire and rescue authority to engage in specialist activities such as rope rescue. A fire and rescue

authority will be able to exercise the power in support of another fire and rescue authority - for example, under a reinforcement scheme (see sections 13 and 14).

30. Section 12 provides a fire and rescue authority with the power to agree to the use of its equipment or personnel for any purpose it believes appropriate and wherever it so chooses. For example, a fire and rescue authority may agree to help pump out a pond as a service to its community.

Assistance in discharge of functions

Sections 13 and 14: Reinforcement schemes and directions as to reinforcement schemes

31. These sections re-enact the existing provisions of the Fire Services Act 1947 on reinforcement schemes and extend them to apply to road traffic accidents and other serious emergencies (as defined by order under section 9). Section 13 obliges fire and rescue authorities to group together, so far as practicable, to provide mutual assistance. If there are cases where fire and rescue authorities are unable to come to an agreement about forming such a group, and one of the authorities concerned requests it, section 14 enables the Secretary of State to direct the fire and rescue authorities involved to make, vary or revoke such a scheme.

32. Before giving a direction, the Secretary of State must give all authorities concerned the opportunity to make representations to him and he may hold an inquiry.

Section 15: Arrangements with other employers of fire-fighters

33. This section extends existing powers in the Fire Services Act 1947 which allow fire and rescue authorities to enter into agreements with organisations that employ their own fire-fighters. For example, if fire-fighters are employed by an airport to respond to plane crashes, an agreement could be entered into so that the airport fire-fighters will respond to and assist with incidents within a certain range of the airport. Fire and rescue authorities could pay the airport for each call that their fire-fighters respond to. These arrangements can also apply to the non-fire emergencies covered by sections 8 and 9. The arrangements under this section cannot be between two fire and rescue authorities as this type of relationship would be covered by sections 13 and 14.

Discharge of functions by others

Sections 16 and 17: Arrangements for discharge of functions by others

34. Section 16 extends existing powers in the Fire Services Act 1947 to provide fire and rescue authorities with the ability to enter into contractual arrangements with others (including other fire and rescue authorities) to provide services in the execution of their functions (covered by sections 6 to 9 and 11). An example would be an agreement where a fire and rescue authority contracts with a local education authority to promote fire safety within its schools. Another example would be where a fire and rescue authority specialises in rope rescue and a neighbouring authority contracts with it to provide some or all of its response to incidents requiring rope rescue.

35. However, a fire and rescue authority can only delegate its fire-fighting functions to another fire and rescue authority or others that employ fire-fighters. An example of such an agreement could be delegating to the licence-holder of a nuclear site, which employs its own

fire service, the responsibility for preparing for, and dealing with, fires within the area of the site.

36. Section 17 re-enacts provisions in the Fire Services Act 1947 that provide the Secretary of State with the ability to require fire and rescue authorities to enter into contractual arrangements under section 16 (or to vary or cancel any such arrangements). The Secretary of State can exercise the power on his own initiative or where one of the authorities has asked him to intervene, but the power must be exercised in the interests of economy, efficiency and effectiveness. Before issuing a direction the Secretary of State must give the fire and rescue authorities affected the opportunity to make representations to him and he may hold an inquiry.

Supplementary

Section 18: Training centres

37. This section re-enacts provisions in the Fire Services Act 1947 that allow a fire and rescue authority to set up and run training centres.

Section 19: Charging

38. Section 19 allows the Secretary of State to set out by order, following consultation, the services for which a fire and rescue authority may charge and the persons who may be subject to the charge. Section 3(1)(e) of the Fire Services Act 1947 already provides fire and rescue authorities with a discretionary power to charge for certain functions. As with the existing legislation, fire and rescue authorities will not be able to charge for extinguishing fires or protecting life and property in the event of fires, except in respect of incidents at sea or under the sea. There is also a prohibition on charging for the provision of emergency medical assistance.

39. Subsection (4) allows any order made under subsection (1) to include a provision for charges to be imposed on, or recovered from, third parties. Subsection (5) maintains the existing arrangement that allows fire and rescue authorities to set their own level of charge, and to vary the charge depending on the type of service provided and the circumstances of a particular incident, or to choose not to charge at all. Subsection (6) limits the amount charged to the cost of providing the service.

Section 20: Exercise of powers at or under sea

40. The Maritime Coastguard Agency (MCA) has a general duty to manage the response of UK authorities to maritime incidents both in territorial waters and beyond. To support such response the MCA will enter into agreements with other service providers. Fire and rescue authorities may indicate to the MCA a willingness to provide a response to fires and other emergencies at sea and to provide fire crews equipped and trained to undertake such work.

41. Section 20 will enable fire and rescue authorities to continue to provide a response to incidents at sea and under the sea.

PART 3: ADMINISTRATION

Fire and Rescue National Framework

Section 21: Fire and Rescue National Framework

42. This section requires the Secretary of State to consult on and prepare a Fire and Rescue National Framework ("the Framework"), to which fire and rescue authorities must have regard in carrying out their functions. The Secretary of State must keep the Framework under review and must consult on any significant revisions made to it. Parliament will have the opportunity to scrutinise the Framework before it takes effect.

43. A draft Framework was published for consultation on 11 December 2003 and the 2004/05 Fire and Rescue National Framework was published on 16 July 2004. The purpose of the Framework is to provide strategic direction from central government while ensuring that authorities continue to make local decisions. The Framework sets out the Government's objectives for the Fire and Rescue Service and what fire and rescue authorities should do to achieve these objectives. The Framework also sets out the support the Government will provide to fire and rescue authorities.

Section 22 and 23: Intervention by Secretary of State and intervention protocol

44. This section gives the Secretary of State the power to intervene if fire and rescue authorities fail to act in accordance with the Framework. The best value powers in Part 1 of the Local Government Act 1999 already make provision for the Secretary of State to intervene where an authority is failing to comply with the requirements of Part 1 of that Act. However, some wider Fire and Rescue Service performance issues covered by the Framework, such as measures to make provision for resilience in the face of a terrorist attack, may not be covered by the 1999 Act.

45. Section 22 provides the Secretary of State with the power to require, by order, a fire and rescue authority to act in accordance with the Framework where he considers that the authority is failing to do so, or is likely to fail to do so. Before making such an order the Secretary of State must give the authority an opportunity to make representations to him.

46. Any use of the Secretary of State's powers under section 22 will be governed by an "intervention protocol". Section 23 requires the Secretary of State to consult on and publish this protocol.

Section 25: Report

47. The Secretary of State will report to Parliament, at least once in every two years, on the extent to which fire and rescue authorities are acting in accordance with the Framework and any action he has taken to ensure they do so. He will not report on individual fire and rescue authorities.

Supervision

Section 26: Information

48. This section applies a power equivalent to section 230 of the Local Government Act 1972 to all fire and rescue authorities and not just those to which section 230 applies. The power could, for example, be used for collecting incident by incident information on primary fires (those involving property, rescues, casualties or fatalities), the number and location of fires

and the number of fire-related casualties and fatalities. This information is in fact already collected from fire and rescue authorities, as is information on false alarms, attendance at road traffic accidents and information on staffing levels. This section formalises the requirement to supply such information.

Section 27: Inquiries

49. Section 27 re-enacts in an amended form section 33 of the Fire Services Act 1947. The Secretary of State will be able to hold an inquiry into the performance of a fire and rescue authority or its handling of a particular incident.

Section 28: Inspectors

50. This section re-enacts the power in the Fire Services Act 1947 that determines the arrangements for appointing inspectors of the Fire and Rescue Service.

Supplementary

Section 29: Equipment, facilities, services and organisations

51. This section enables the Secretary of State to provide equipment, services and facilities to fire and rescue authorities, to maintain anything so provided or to contribute towards the cost of such provision or maintenance. For example, this section gives the Secretary of State authority to provide equipment to prepare authorities to deal with civil resilience incidents and to provide standardised systems for radio communications and control rooms. This will help to ensure consistency of approach in the case of major emergencies, such as a terrorist incident.

52. Section 29 empowers the Secretary of State to establish and maintain any organisation he considers appropriate if it promotes the economy, efficiency or effectiveness of authorities or to contribute towards the costs of such an organisation. Where he establishes or maintains such an organisation or provides anything under this section, authorities may be charged for the use of the associated equipment, facilities and services.

53. This section also allows the Secretary of State, by order following consultation, to require authorities to use specified services or to use and maintain specified equipment and facilities.

Section 30: Directions for public safety purposes

54. This section provides the Secretary of State with the power to give directions, by order, to fire and rescue authorities as to the use and disposal of their property or facilities for the purposes of public safety. Such a direction may cover all kinds of property and facilities, whether or not they have been provided as part of a national procurement exercise under section 29. An example of when this power might be used is during a period of industrial action when emergency cover provided by a fire and rescue authority is insufficient and in order to ensure public safety their equipment needs to be used by others providing emergency cover.

Section 31: Training institution and centres

55. The Act provides for training for fire and rescue authority employees (and others) to be delivered centrally, regionally or locally. This section re-enacts and enhances provision allowing the Secretary of State to set up and maintain central or local (including regional) training centres.

56. The Fire Service College at Moreton in Marsh is the central training institution for the Fire and Rescue Service. It provides specialist, operational incident and New Dimension training which is considered most effectively delivered at a national level. Other training (for example, that which needs to be carried out regularly) is considered best delivered at a regional or local level.

PART 4: EMPLOYMENT

Negotiating bodies

Section 32 Negotiating bodies

57. Section 32 provides the Secretary of State with reserve powers to establish negotiating machinery for the Fire and Rescue Service. The powers allow the Secretary of State to determine the number, composition and chair of the negotiating bodies following consultation.

58. Subsection (2) requires that a statutory body includes employers and employee representative bodies and an independent chairman. No member or employee of a fire and rescue authority, employee representative body, civil service or a Minister may serve as the chairman.

59. Should any negotiating body be set up under these powers, subsections (4) and (5) would prevent the body being undermined by negotiations being held in another forum. Subsections (5) to (8) however would allow the statutory body to make arrangements for certain conditions of service to be negotiated locally (either in their entirety or within nationally agreed parameters).

Section 33: Guidance

60. Section 33 allows the Secretary of State to issue guidance to negotiating bodies. Any negotiating body, whether established voluntarily or under section 32, would be required to have regard to the guidance issued to them.

Pensions etc.

Section 34: Pensions etc.

61. This section re-enacts existing powers in section 26 of the Fire Services Act 1947. It will enable more than one pension scheme to operate at any one time. This section also allows a range of financial arrangements for funding these schemes.

Section 35: Information in connection with pensions etc.

62. This section re-enacts provisions in the Fire Services Act 1947 which enable the Secretary of State to prescribe the circumstances in which a fire and rescue authority or a Scottish fire authority may provide information to a person who has opted or transferred out of any pension scheme for fire-fighters. It also re-enacts the existing provisions about charging for administrative expenses.

Section 36: Preservation of existing pension scheme

63. Pension arrangements for fire-fighters are currently provided by the Firemen's Pension Scheme Order 1992 (S.I. 1992/129 as amended) made under section 26 of the Fire Services

Act 1947. The purpose of section 36 is to ensure that the scheme can continue in operation despite the repeal of the 1947 Act and to enable the 1992 Order to be modified.

Supplementary

Section 37: Prohibition on employment of police

64. This section re-enacts section 32 of the Fire Services Act 1947 and provides that no member of a police force (i.e. a police constable) may be employed as a fire-fighter. If an off-duty police officer were employed by a fire and rescue authority, for example as a retained (part-time) fire-fighter, difficulties might arise at the scene of a fire or other emergency due to confusion over which employer had the primary claim on the officer's services.

PART 5: WATER SUPPLY

Section 38: Duty to secure water supply etc.

65. Subsection (1) re-enacts section 13 of the Fire Services Act 1947, requiring fire and rescue authorities to take all reasonable measures to ensure the adequate supply of water for use in the event of fire.

66. Subsection (2) allows an authority to use any suitable supply of water, whether provided by a water undertaker or any other person. Whilst it provides for payment of reasonable compensation for the water, this is limited by reference to section 147 of the Water Industry Act 1991, which expressly forbids charging by a water undertaker in respect of: water taken for the purpose of extinguishing fires or for any other emergency purposes; water taken for testing apparatus used for extinguishing fires; or for fire-fighting training. This subsection re-enacts section 15(1) of the 1947 Act.

Section 39: Supply of water by water undertakers

67. This section re-enacts section 14(1) and (4) of the Fire Services Act 1947 Act and allows a fire and rescue authority to enter into an agreement with a water undertaker for the supply of water (as covered by section 37). Subsection (2) allows for any agreement to include terms for payment, other than for the purposes covered by section 147 of the Water Industry Act 1991.

68. Subsection (4) makes any obligation of a water undertaker, under an agreement, enforceable by the Secretary of State under section 18 of the Water Industry Act 1991. This gives the Secretary of State power to make an enforcement order to secure compliance with any statutory or other requirement.

Section 40: Emergency supply by water undertaker

69. This section re-enacts sections 30(4) and 30(4)(a) of the Fire Services Act 1947. Subsection (1) places an obligation on a water undertaker to take all necessary steps to increase supply and pressure of water for the purpose of extinguishing a fire, if requested to do so by a fire and rescue authority. Subsection (2) allows a water undertaker to shut off water from the mains and pipes in any area to enable it to comply with a request to increase supply and water pressure. Subsection (3) safeguards the fire and rescue authority or any person from any liability for anything done by a water undertaker in complying with its obligations. Subsections (4) and (5) make it an offence for a water undertaker, without

reasonable excuse, to fail to take any steps which it is obliged to take and provides for a level 5 fine (currently £5,000) on summary conviction.

Section 41: Supply by other persons

70. This section re-enacts section 15(1) of the Fire Services Act 1947 and allows a fire and rescue authority to enter into agreements with persons other than water undertakers in order to secure the use of water; to improve access to water; or to lay and maintain pipes and to carry out other works in connection with the use of water.

Section 42: Fire hydrants

71. Access to the water supply is by connection to a fire hydrant. Hydrants may be fitted by a water undertaker at the request of a fire and rescue authority. Section 41(1) requires a water undertaker to mark the location of every fire hydrant with a notice or distinguishing mark and under subsection (3) the costs of doing this can be charged to the fire and rescue authority in whose area the hydrant is situated. This re-enacts provisions in section 14(3) of the Fire Services Act 1947.

72. Subsection (4) enables the Secretary of State to make regulations providing for uniformity in fire hydrants and the distinguishing notices and marks indicating their location. This re-enacts section 14(6) of the 1947 Act.

73. Subsection (5) makes any obligation of a water undertaker under subsection (1) and (4) enforceable by the Secretary of State under section 18 of the Water Industry Act 1991, which gives the Secretary of State power to make an enforcement order to secure compliance with any statutory or other requirement. This re-enacts section 14(4) of the 1947 Act.

74. Subsection (6) makes it an offence for any person to use a fire hydrant other than for the purpose of fire-fighting or any other purpose of a fire and rescue authority; or other than for any purpose authorised by the water undertaker or other person to whom the hydrant belongs.

75. Subsection (7) makes it an offence to damage or obstruct a fire hydrant. Under subsection (8) a person guilty of an offence under subsection (6) and (7) is liable on summary conviction to a level 2 fine. Subsections (6), (7) and (8) re-enact section 14(5) of the 1947 Act.

Section 43: Notice of works affecting water supply and fire hydrants

76. This section re-enacts section 16(1) to (3) of the Fire Services Act 1947 and requires any person who proposes to carry out any works for the purpose of supplying water to any part of the area of a fire and rescue authority to give at least six weeks' written notice to the authority. A person proposing to carry out any works affecting a fire hydrant is required to give at least seven days' notice in writing.

77. Under subsection (3), if it is not practicable for written notice to be given, the person is regarded as having given such notice if he gives it as soon as practicable. It is an offence under subsection (4) if, without reasonable excuse, a person fails to give notice as required. Under subsection (5) a person is liable on summary conviction to a level 5 fine.

PART 6: SUPPLEMENTARY

Powers in the event of emergency

Section 44: Powers of fire-fighters etc in an emergency

78. This provision provides individual authorised employees of a fire and rescue authority with the powers to deal with fires (which have either broken out or situations where a fire fighter reasonably believes a fire is about to break out), road traffic accidents and other emergencies. It replaces section 30(1) of the Fire Services Act 1947 which was limited to dealing with extinguishing, or preventing the spread of, fires and recognises the wider range of duties of fire-fighters including the work which fire and rescue authorities do in responding to road traffic accidents.

Powers of entry

Section 45: Obtaining information and investigating fires

79. This section allows an authorised employee of a fire and rescue authority to enter premises to obtain information that is needed for the discharge of the core functions of fire fighting (section 7), dealing with road traffic accidents (section 8) and specified emergencies (section 9). In the case of premises where a fire has occurred, the section also allows an authorised employee to gain entry in order to investigate the cause and progression of the fire that has occurred there. Such entry cannot be forcible and 24 hours notice must be given to the occupier of a private dwelling, unless authorised by a justice of the peace.

Section 46: Supplementary powers

80. Section 46 sets out the powers and the obligations of an employee of a fire and rescue authority who has entered premises under section 45 to gain information or investigate the cause and progression of a fire. The powers and obligations are similar to those applicable to investigations under health and safety legislation.

Section 47: Notices: general

81. Section 47 provides for the service of notices under section 45 . It is similar to service provisions under fire safety and health and safety law.

Section 48: Notices given electronically

82. Section 48 provides for the electronic service of notices where the recipient agrees to this.

False alarms

Section 49: False alarms of fire

83. Section 49 re-enacts section 31 of the Fire Services Act 1947. This section provides that a person who knowingly gives or causes someone else to give a false alarm of fire to a person acting on behalf of a fire and rescue authority is liable to a maximum level 4 fine, prison sentence of 51 weeks, or both.

Consequential provision

Section 51: Abolition of Central Fire Brigades Advisory Council

84. Section 51 abolishes the Central Fire Brigades Advisory Council, which was established under section 29 of the Fire Services Act 1947 to provide general advice to the Secretary of State on matters relating to the operation of that Act. The Council also served as statutory consultee prior to the exercise by the Secretary of State of certain of his regulation-making powers under the 1947 Act (for example with regard to pensions). Where such regulation-making powers are re-enacted elsewhere in the Act, the Secretary of State will be under a duty to consult with such persons he considers appropriate.

PART 7: GENERAL

Sections 62 and 63: Wales/Extent

85. The Act generally applies to England and Wales only. However, as pension policy is a reserved matter under the Scotland Act 1998, the provisions regarding pensions in Part 4 and various consequential provisions also extend to Scotland.

86. In its application to Wales, the Act gives the National Assembly for Wales the powers of the Secretary of State as set out in sections 2 to 4, 9, 10, 14, 17, 19, 21 to 23, 26 to 34, 36, 42, 50, 53, 60 and 61.

87. The provision for the National Assembly to prepare, following consultation, a National Framework for the Fire and Rescue Service in Wales will be brought into effect by order subject to the usual Assembly arrangements for statutory instruments. Rather than a requirement to report to Parliament on the Framework, as is the case in England (under section 25), the Assembly is required to "publish a report".

COMMENCEMENT

88. Section 61 contains provisions relating to the coming into force of the Act. Sections 55-64 came into force on Royal Assent. The remaining provisions come into force on such dates as the Secretary of State or the National Assembly for Wales by order appoint.

HANSARD REFERENCES

The following table sets out the dates and Hansard references for each stage of this Act's passage through Parliament.

Stage	Date	Hansard Reference
House of Commons		
Introduction	12 January 2004	Vol. 416 Col 531
Second Reading	26 January 2004	Vol. 417 Col 40
Committee	10 February - 2 March 2004	Hansard Standing Committee G
Report and Third Reading	15 March 2004	Vol. 419 Col 21

These notes refer to the Fire and Rescue Services Act 2004 (c.21)
which received Royal Assent on Thursday 22 July 2004

	15 March 2004	Vol. 419 Col 111
House of Lords		
Introduction	16 March 2004	Vol. 659 Col 138
Second reading	6 April 2004	Vol. 659 Col 1777
Grand Committee	6 May 2004	Vol. 660 Col GC 237
	11 May 2004	Vol. 661 Col GC 61
	19 May 2004	Vol. 661 Col GC 335
	24 May 2004	Vol. 661 Col GC 401
Report	12 July 2004	Vol. 663 Col 1015
Third Reading	20 July 2004	Vol. 664 Col 111
House of Commons		
Commons Consideration of Lords Amendments	21 July 2004	Vol. 124 Col 433

Royal Assent - 22 July 2004   House of Commons Vol. 424 Col 514

House of Lords Vol. 664 Col 333

Printed in the UK by The Stationery Office Limited
under the authority and superintendence of Carol Tullo, Controller of
Her Majesty's Stationery Office and Queen's Printer of Acts of Parliament.

Published by TSO (The Stationery Office) and available from:

Online
www.tso.co.uk/bookshop

Mail, Telephone, Fax & E-mail
TSO
PO Box 29, Norwich NR3 1GN
Telephone orders/General enquiries 0870 600 5522
Fax orders 0870 600 5533
Order through the Parliamentary Hotline *Lo-call* 0845 7 023474
Email book.orders@tso.co.uk
Textphone 0870 240 3701

TSO Shops
123 Kingsway, London WC2B 6PQ
020 7242 6393 Fax 020 7242 6394
68–69 Bull Street, Birmingham B4 6AD
0121 236 9696 Fax 0121 236 9699
9–21 Princess Street, Manchester M60 8AS
0161 834 7201 Fax 0161 833 0634
16 Arthur Street, Belfast BT1 4GD
028 9023 8451 Fax 028 9023 5401
18–19 High Street, Cardiff CF10 1PT
029 2039 5548 Fax 029 2038 4347
71 Lothian Road, Edinburgh EH3 9AZ
0870 606 5566 Fax 0870 606 5588

The Parliamentary Bookshop
12 Bridge Street, Parliament Square,
London SW1A 2JX
Telephone orders/General enquiries 020 7219 3890
Fax orders 020 7219 3866

Accredited Agents
(see Yellow Pages)

and through good booksellers

ISBN 0-10-562104-8

9 780105 621041